crocodile
stitch
fashions™

contents

Triangle
Shawl

SKILL LEVEL

INTERMEDIATE

FINISHED SIZE
24 x 59 inches

MATERIALS
- Universal Yarn Swiss Mohair super fine (fingering) weight yarn (3½ oz/601 yds/100g per skein): 3 skeins #2502 edelweiss
- Size I/9/5.5mm crochet hook or size needed to obtain gauge

1 SUPER FINE

GAUGE
3 V-sts = 2 inches; 7 V-st rows = 4 inches

PATTERN NOTES
Mohair is quite a challenging yarn to pull out, which can be particularly frustrating when learning a new stitch. To make your crochet experience pleasant, first make a swatch of the pattern using yarn of your preference until you become confident with the crocodile stitch. It will not take long for you to master it.

Gauge is not important for this project. The choice of a large hook is intentional to provide better drape for the Shawl.

The shawl is worked from the bottom up. This type of construction gives you freedom to choose Shawl size of your preference. A neck warmer, a medium or a large shawl are all possible size variations with this single pattern.

If making larger Shawl, you may need more yarn than stated in Materials.

If making smaller Shawl, you may not use all the yarn stated in Materials.

In short, the crocodile stitch is formed by a two-row repeat: a row of V-stitches followed by a row of scales (or shells). This is a fairly easy pattern to execute and is fast to memorize. The only novelty about this design is that the scales are crocheted in front of the V-stitches with clusters of front post double crochets from top to bottom, then from bottom to top, as opposed to working them on top of the row like most shell patterns.

The first scale is worked in a round that is not joined; the remainder of the pattern is worked in rows. Each row of scales will increase the number of scales by one, forming the triangular shape.

Photos used are worked with larger hook and yarn in order to show more detail.

Chain-3 at beginning of row or round counts as first double crochet unless otherwise stated.

Chain-4 at beginning of row or round counts as first double crochet and chain-1 unless otherwise stated.

Join with slip stitch as indicated unless otherwise stated.

SPECIAL STITCH
V-stitch (V-st): (Dc, ch 1, dc) as indicated in instructions.

INSTRUCTIONS
SHAWL
Rnd 1 (RS): Ch 6, sl st in first ch to form ring, **ch 3** *(see Pattern Notes)*, 11 dc in ring, **do not join or turn.**

This first open rnd counts as the first scale and bottom point of the Shawl.

Row 2 (WS): Now working in rows, **ch 4** *(see Pattern Notes)*, dc in same st as beg ch *(counts as first V-st of row)*, **V-st** *(see Special Stitch)* in ring, V-st in last st *(see photo A)*, turn.

A

C

Row 3: Ch 3, working from top to bottom around post of first dc of first V-st, work 5 **fpdc** *(see Stitch Guide and photo B)*, turn work so V-st is sideways and post of 2nd dc of V-st is upside down *(V point of V-st will be facing right, see photo C)*, working from bottom to top around post of 2nd dc of V-st, work 6 fpdc *(see photo D)*, sk next V-st, working from top to bottom, work 6 fpdc around post of first dc of last V-st, turn work so V-st is sideways, working from bottom to top around post of 2nd dc of V-st, work 6 fpdc, turn *(see photo E)*.

D

B

E

Row 4: Ch 4, dc in same st as beg ch *(count as first V-st of row)*, V-st in next ch-1 sp, yo, insert hook in both next ch-1 sp and in sp between scales directly behind ch-1 sp *(see photo F1 and F2)*, complete V-st, V-st in next ch-1 sp, V-st in last st *(see photo G)*, turn.

F1

F2

G

Row 5: Ch 3, working from top to bottom around post of first dc of first V-st, work 5 fpdc, turn work so V-st is sideways and post of 2nd dc of V-st is upside down, working from bottom to top around post of 2nd dc of V-st, work 6 fpdc, *sk next V-st, working from top to bottom around post of first dc of next V-st, work 6 fpdc, turn work so V-st is sideways, working from bottom to top around post of 2nd dc of V-st, work 6 fpdc, rep from * across, turn.

Row 6: Ch 4, dc in same st as beg ch *(count as first V-st of row)*, V-st in next ch-1 sp, *yo, insert hook in both next ch-1 sp and in sp between scales directly behind ch-1 sp, complete V-st, V-st in next ch-1 sp, rep from * across to last st, V-st in last st, turn.

Next rows: Rep rows 5 and 6 alternately until desired length is reached, ending with row 6. At end of last row, fasten off.

The Shawl in photo has 25 reps.

FRINGE
Cut 6 strands, each 14 inches in length.

Holding all strands tog, fold in half. Pull fold through as stated, pull ends through fold. Pull to tighten.

Attach Fringe in sps between scales along sides and in first st at upper corner, leaving upper edge without Fringe. Trim ends. ■

Crocodile Stitch Hood

SKILL LEVEL

INTERMEDIATE

FINISHED SIZE

Cowl section: 7 inches wide x 24 inches circumference

Hood section: 11 inches wide x 12 inches high

MATERIALS

- Universal Yarn Uptown DK (light) weight yarn (3½ oz/273 yds/100g per skein):
  2½ skeins #128 latte
- Size G/6/4mm crochet hook or size needed to obtain gauge
- Tapestry needle
- Stitch marker

GAUGE

Dc rib pattern: 8 dc = 2 inches; 4 dc rows = 2 inches

PATTERN NOTES

Hood is worked in 2 pieces, hood and cowl, that are sewn together.

In short, the crocodile stitch is formed by a two-row repeat: a row of V-stitches followed by a row of scales (or shells). This is a fairly easy pattern to execute and is fast to memorize. The only novelty about this design is that the scales are crocheted in front of the V-stitches with clusters of front post double crochets from top to bottom, then from bottom to top, as opposed to working them on top of the row like in most shell patterns.

Photos used are worked with larger hook and yarn in order to show more detail.

Chain-3 at beginning of row or round counts as first double crochet unless otherwise stated.

Do not join or turn rounds unless otherwise stated.

Mark first stitch of round.

Chain-4 at beginning of row or round counts as first double crochet and chain-1 unless otherwise stated.

Join with slip stitch as indicated unless otherwise stated.

SPECIAL STITCH

V-stitch (V-st): (Dc, ch 1, dc) as indicated in instructions.

INSTRUCTIONS
HOOD
COWL SECTION

Rnd 1: Ch 102, being careful not to twist chain, sl st in first ch to form ring, **ch 4** *(see Pattern Notes)*, dc in same st as beg ch, *sk next 2 chs, **V-st** *(see Special Stitch)* in next ch, rep from * around, **join** *(see Pattern Notes)* in 3rd ch of beg ch-4. *(34 V-sts)*

Rnd 2: **Ch 3** *(see Pattern Notes)*, working from top to bottom around post of first dc of first V-st, work 4 **fpdc** *(see Stitch Guide and photo A)*, ch 1, turn work so V-st is sideways and post of 2nd dc of V-st is upside down *(V point of V-st will be facing right, see photo B)*, working from bottom to top around post of 2nd dc of V-st, work 5 fpdc *(see photo C1 and C2)*, *sk next V-st, working from top to bottom, work 5 fpdc around post of first dc of next V-st, ch 1, turn work so V-st is sideways, working from bottom to top around post of 2nd dc of V-st, work 5 fpdc, rep from * around, join in 3rd ch of beg ch-3. *(17 scales)*

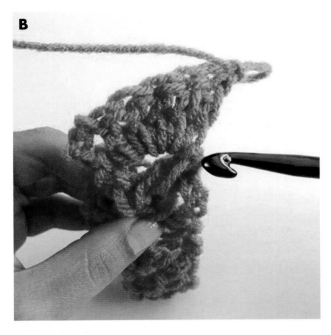

B

A

C1

C2

D2

Rnd 3: Sl st in each of first 2 sts, sl st in ch-1 sp, ch 4, dc in same ch-1 sp, yo, insert hook in next sp between scales and in ch-1 sp directly behind scales, complete as V-st *(see photo D1 and D2)*, * V-st in next ch-1 sp, yo, insert hook in next sp between scales and in ch-1 sp directly behind scales, complete as V-st, rep from * around, join in 3rd ch of beg ch-4. *(34 V-sts)*

D1

Rnd 4: Sl st in first ch-1 sp, working from top to bottom around post of first dc of next V-st, work 5 fpdc, ch 1, turn work so V-st is sideways and post of 2nd dc of V-st is upside down, working from bottom to top around post of second dc of V-st, work 5 fpdc, *sk next V-st, working from top to bottom around post of first dc of next V-st, work 5 fpdc, ch 1, turn work so V-st is sideways, working from bottom to top around post of 2nd dc of V-st, work 5 fpdc, rep from * around; join in top of first fpdc. *(17 scales)*

Rnds 5–10: [Rep rnds 3 and 4 alternately] 3 times.

Row 11: Now working in rows, ch 3, *dc in each of next 2 sts, dc in next ch-1 sp, dc in each of next 2 sts, **Yo, insert hook** in next sp between scales and in ch-1 sp directly behind scales, yo, pull lp through and complete as dc, rep from * across, **do not join, turn.** *(102 dc)*

Rows 12–17: Ch 3, working in **back lps** *(see Stitch Guide)*, dc in each st across, turn.

Continue working in rows without joining for rib section to be sewn together at Finishing.

Last row: Ch 3, working in back lps, dc in each st across. Leaving long end for sewing, fasten off.

HOOD SECTION

Row 1: Ch 94, dc in 4th ch from hook, dc in each ch across, turn. *(91 dc)*

Rows 2–16: Ch 3 , working in **back lps** *(see Stitch Guide)*, dc in each dc across, turn.

Row 17 (WS): Ch 3, [sk next 2 dc, V-st in next dc] across to last dc, dc in last dc, turn. *(2 dc, 29 V-sts)*

Row 18 (RS): Ch 1, working from top to bottom around post of first dc of first V-st, work 5 fpdc, ch 1, turn work so V-st is sideways and post of 2nd dc of V-st is upside down *(V point of V-st will be facing right)*, working from bottom to top around post of 2nd dc of V-st, work 5 fpdc, *sk next V-st, working from top to bottom around post of first dc of next V-st, work 5 fpdc, ch 1, turn work so V-st is sideways, working from bottom to top around post of 2nd dc of V-st, work 5 fpdc, rep from * across to last dc, sl st in last dc, turn. *(15 scales)*

Row 19: Ch 3, V-st in next ch-1 sp, *yo, insert hook in next ch-1 sp and in sp between scales directly behind ch-1 sp, complete as V-st, V-st in next ch-1 sp, rep from * across to last dc, dc in last st, turn. *(29 V-sts)*

Row 20: Sl st in each of first 2 sts, sl st in next ch-1 sp, working from top to bottom around post of first dc of next V-st, work 5 fpdc, ch 1, turn work so V-st is sideways and post of 2nd dc of V-st is upside down, working from bottom to top around post of 2nd dc of V-st, work 5 fpdc, *sk next V-st, working from top to bottom around post of first dc of next V-st, work 5 fpdc, ch 1, turn work so V-st is sideways, working from bottom to top around post of 2nd dc of V-st, work 5 fpdc, rep from * across to last V-st, sl st in next ch-1 sp, sl st in each of last 2 sts, turn. *(14 scales)*

Row 21: Ch 3, V-st in ch-1 sp of first V-st, *V-st in next ch-1 sp, yo, insert hook in next ch-1 sp and in sp between scales directly behind ch-1 sp, complete as V-st, V-st in next ch-1 sp, rep from * across to last ch-1 sp, V-st in last ch-1 sp, dc in last st, turn. *(29 V-sts)*

Rows 22–26: [Rep rows 18–21 consecutively for pattern] twice, ending last rep with row 18.

Last row: Ch 1 *(counts as first sc)*, *sc in each of next 2 sts, sc in next ch-1 sp, sc in each of next 2 sts, **sc dec** *(see Stitch Guide)* in next ch-1 sp and in sp between scales directly behind ch-1 st, rep from * across to last 4 sts, sc in each of the last 4 sts. Fasten off.

FINISHING

With WS facing, fold Hood in half lengthwise and sew along ribbed edge (opposite edge from scales). Sew ribbed section edges of Cowl tog. With WS facing, sew Cowl to Hood along bottom edge of Hood as shown in photo E. ■

E

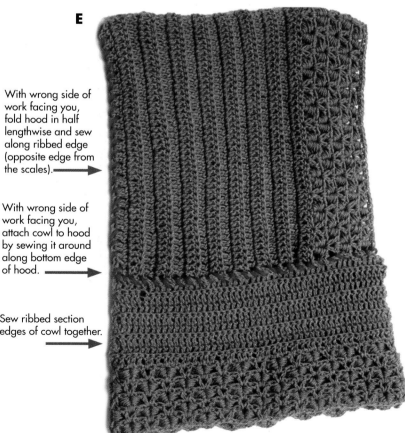

With wrong side of work facing you, fold hood in half lengthwise and sew along ribbed edge (opposite edge from the scales).

With wrong side of work facing you, attach cowl to hood by sewing it around along bottom edge of hood.

Sew ribbed section edges of cowl together.

Wrist Warmers

SKILL LEVEL

INTERMEDIATE

FINISHED SIZES

Small/medium and large

MATERIALS

- Premier Yarns Deborah Norville Serenity Sock Weight Solids super fine (fingering) weight yarn (1¾ oz/230 yds/50g per skein): 2 skeins #DN150-11 charcoal
- Size crochet hook needed for size and to obtain gauge

GAUGE

Small/medium size using size E/4/3.5mm hook: 12 V-sts = 2 inches; 5 V-st rows = 2 inches

Large size using size F/5/3.75mm hook: 10 V-sts = 2 inches; 9 V-st rows = 4 inches

PATTERN NOTES

Wrist Warmers are crocheted from hand to cuff.

In short, the crocodile stitch is formed by a two-row repeat: a row of V-stitches followed by a row of scales (or shells). This is a fairly easy pattern to execute and is fast to memorize. The only novelty about this design is that the scales are crocheted in front of the V-stitches with clusters of front post double crochets from top to bottom, then from bottom to top, as opposed to working them on top of the row like in most shell patterns.

Photos used are worked with larger hook and yarn in order to show more detail.

Chain-3 at beginning of row or round counts as first double crochet unless otherwise stated.

Chain-4 at beginning of row or round counts as first double crochet and chain-1 unless otherwise stated.

Join with slip stitch as indicated unless otherwise stated.

SPECIAL STITCH

V-stitch (V-st): (Dc, ch 1, dc) as indicated in instructions.

INSTRUCTIONS
WRIST WARMER
MAKE 2.

Rnd 1: Ch 42, being careful not to twist chain, sl st in first ch to form ring, **ch 4** (see Pattern Notes), dc in same stitch as beg ch, *sk next 2 chs, **V-st** (see Special Stitch) in next ch, rep from * around, **join** (see Pattern Notes) in 3rd ch of beg ch-4. (14 V-sts)

Rnd 2: Ch 3 (see Pattern Notes), working from top to bottom around post of first dc of first V-st, work 4 **fpdc** (see Stitch Guide and see photo A on page 16), ch 1, turn work so V-st is sideways and post of 2nd dc of V-st is upside down (V point of V-st will be facing right, see photo B on page 16), working from bottom to top around post of 2nd dc of V-st, work 5 fpdc (see photo C1 and C2 on page 16), *sk next V-st, working from top to bottom, work 5 fpdc around post of first dc of next V-st, ch 1, turn work so V-st is sideways, working from bottom to top around post of 2nd dc of V-st, work 5 fpdc, rep from * around, join in 3rd ch of beg ch-3. (7 scales)

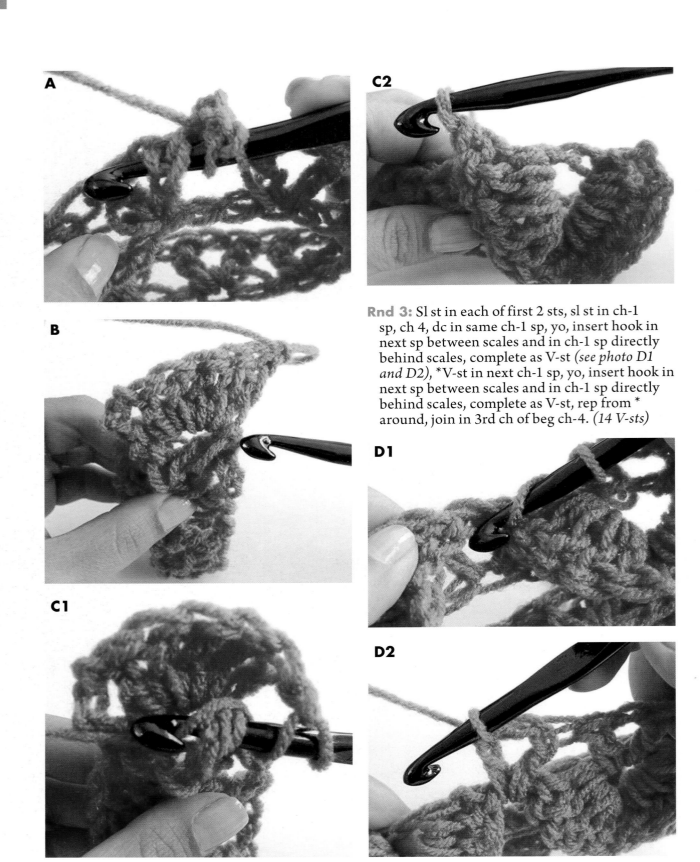

A

B

C1

C2

Rnd 3: Sl st in each of first 2 sts, sl st in ch-1 sp, ch 4, dc in same ch-1 sp, yo, insert hook in next sp between scales and in ch-1 sp directly behind scales, complete as V-st *(see photo D1 and D2)*, *V-st in next ch-1 sp, yo, insert hook in next sp between scales and in ch-1 sp directly behind scales, complete as V-st, rep from * around, join in 3rd ch of beg ch-4. *(14 V-sts)*

D1

D2

Rnd 4: Sl st in ch-1 sp, working from top to bottom around post of first dc of next V-st, work 5 fpdc, ch 1, turn work so V-st is sideways and post of 2nd dc of V-st is upside down, working from bottom to top around post of 2nd dc of V-st, work 5 fpdc, *sk next V-st, working from top to bottom around post of first dc of next V-st, work 5 fpdc, ch 1, turn work so V-st is sideways, working from bottom to top around post of 2nd dc of V-st, work 5 fpdc, rep from * around, join in beg fpdc. *(7 scales)*

Rnds 5–14: [Rep rnds 3 and 4 alternately for pattern] 5 times.

Rnd 15: Ch 3, *dc dec *(see Stitch Guide)* in next 2 sts, dc in next ch-1 sp, dc dec in next 2 sts, yo, insert hook in next sp between scales and in ch-1 sp directly behind scales, yo, pull lp through, complete as dc, rep from * around, join in 3rd ch of beg ch-3. *(28 dc)*

Rnds 16 & 17: Ch 3, dc in each st around, join in 3rd ch of beg ch-3.

Rnd 18: Ch 3, dc in each of next 4 dc, dc dec in next 2 sts, [dc in each of next 5 dc, dc dec in next 2 dc] around, join in 3rd ch of beg ch-3. *(24 dc)*

Rnds 19–26: Ch 3, dc in each st around, join 3rd ch of beg ch-3.

Rnd 27: Ch 3, dc in each of next 4 dc, 2 dc in next dc, [dc in each of next 5 dc, 2 dc in next dc] around, join in 3rd ch of beg ch-3. *(28 dc)*

Rnds 28–37: Ch 3, dc in each st around, join in 3rd ch of beg ch-3. At end of last row, fasten off. ■

Flapper Hat

SKILL LEVEL

INTERMEDIATE

FINISHED SIZE
20–22-inch head circumference

MATERIALS
- Universal Yarn Uptown DK light (DK) weight yarn (3½ oz/ 273 yds/100g per skein): 2 skeins #131 granite
- Size G/6/4mm crochet hook or size needed to obtain gauge
- Tapestry needle
- ⅞-inch buttons: 2
- Stitch marker

GAUGE
8 sc = 2 inches; 9 sc rows = 2 inches

PATTERN NOTES
The Hat and 2 Flaps are crocheted separately and then sewn together.

In short, the crocodile stitch is formed by a two-row repeat: a row of V-stitches followed by a row of scales (or shells). This is a fairly easy pattern to execute and is fast to memorize. The only novelty about this design is that the scales are crocheted in front of the V-stitches with clusters of front post double crochets from top to bottom, then from bottom to top, as opposed to working them on top of the row like in most shell patterns.

Photos used are worked with larger hook and yarn in order to show more detail.

Chain-3 at beginning of row or round counts as first double crochet unless otherwise stated.

Do not join or turn rounds unless otherwise stated.

Mark first stitch of round.

Chain-4 at beginning of row or round counts as first double crochet and chain-1 unless otherwise stated.

Join with slip stitch as indicated unless otherwise stated.

SPECIAL STITCH
V-stitch (V-st): (Dc, ch 1, dc) as indicated in instructions.

HAT
Rnd 1: Ch 3, sl st in first ch to form ring, ch 1, 7 sc in ring, **do not join** (see Pattern Notes). (7 sc)

Rnd 2: 2 sc in each sc around. (14 sc)

Rnd 3: [Sc in next sc, 2 sc in next sc] around. (21 sc)

Rnd 4: [Sc in each of next 2 sc, 2 sc in next sc] around. (28 sc)

Rnd 5: [Sc in each of next 3 sc, 2 sc in next sc] around. (35 sc)

Rnd 6: [Sc in each of next 4 sc, 2 sc in next sc] around. (42 sc)

Rnd 7: [Sc in each of next 5 sc, 2 sc on next sc] around. (49 sc)

Rnd 8: [Sc in each of next 6 sc, 2 sc in next sc] around. (56 sc)

Rnd 9: [Sc in each of next 7 sc, 2 sc in next sc] around. (63 sc)

Rnd 10: [Sc in each of next 8 sc, 2 sc in next sc] around. (70 sc)

Rnd 11: [Sc in each of next 9 sc, 2 sc in next sc] around. *(77 sc)*

Rnd 12: [Sc in each of next 10 sc, 2 sc in next sc] around. *(84 sc)*

Rnds 13–35: Sc in each sc around. At end of last rnd, fasten off.

FLAP
MAKE 2.
Rnd 1: Ch 6, sl st in first ch to form ring, **ch 3** *(see Pattern Notes)*, 4 dc in ring, ch 1, 5 dc in ring. **Do not join round, and do not turn.**

This first open rnd counts as the first scale of the Flap.

Row 2: Now working in rows, **ch 4** *(see Pattern Notes)*, dc in same st as beg ch, **V-st** *(see Special Stitch)* in ring, V-st in last st, turn *(see photo A)*.

B1

B2

A

C

Row 3: Ch 3, working from top to bottom around post of first dc of first V-st, work 4 **fpdc** *(see Stitch Guide and photo B1 and B2)*, ch 1, turn work so V-st is sideways and post of 2nd dc of V-st is upside down *(V point of V-st will be facing right, see photo C)*, working from bottom to top around post of 2nd dc of V-st, work 5 fpdc *(see photo D on page 22)*, sk next V-st, working from top to bottom, work 5 fpdc around post of first dc of last V-st, ch 1, turn work so V-st is sideways, working from bottom to top around post of 2nd dc of V-st, work 5 fpdc *(see photo E on page 22)*, turn.

D

F2

E

Row 4: Ch 4, dc in same st as beg ch, V-st in next ch-1 sp, yo, insert hook in next ch-1 sp and in sp between scales directly behind ch-1 sp (see photo F1 and F2), complete as V-st, V-st in next ch-1 sp, V-st in last st, turn.

F1

Row 5: Ch 3, working from top to bottom around post of first dc of first V-st, work 4 fpdc, ch 1, turn work so V-st is sideways and post of 2nd dc of V-st is upside down, working from bottom to top around post of 2nd dc of V-st, work 5 fpdc, *sk next V-st, working from top to bottom around post of first dc of next V-st, work 5 fpdc, ch 1, turn work so V-st is sideways, working from bottom to top around post of 2nd dc of V-st, work 5 fpdc, rep from * across, turn.

Row 6: Ch 4, dc in same st as beg ch, V-st in next ch-1 sp, *yo, insert hook in both next ch-1 sp and in sp between scales directly behind ch-1 sp, complete as V-st, V-st in next ch-1 sp, rep from * across to last st, V-st in last st, turn.

Rows 7–13: [Rep rows 5 and 6 alternately for pattern] 4 times, ending last rep with row 5, which is row of scales.

Last row: Ch 1, sc in each of next 2 sts, sc in next ch-1 sp, sc in each of next 2 sts, *insert hook in next sp between scales and in ch-1 sp directly behind scales, yo, pull lp through and complete as sc, sc in each of next 2 sts, sc in next ch-1 sp, sc in each of next 2 sts, rep from * across. Fasten off.

FINISHING

Flatten Hat, side against side. With WS of Flap facing, sew long edge of Flap to bottom edge of Hat *(see photo G)*.

Button should be placed in the middle of each side of the Hat, measuring 9½ inches from the point of the flap *(see photo H)*.

Turn Hat over and rep with rem Flap.

The center sp of first scale of each Flap will work as buttonholes *(see photo I)*. ∎

Crocodile Stitch Cloche

SKILL LEVEL

INTERMEDIATE

FINISHED SIZE
20–22 inches head circumference

MATERIALS
- Universal Yarn Uptown Baby Sport fine (sport) weight yarn (3½ oz/361 yds/100g per skein): 1 skein #204 shell
- Size G/6/4mm crochet hook or size needed to obtain gauge
- Tapestry needle
- Stitch marker

GAUGE
3 V-sts = 2 inches; 4 V-st rows = 2 inches

PATTERN NOTES
Cloche is worked in rounds beginning at lower edge.

In short, the crocodile stitch is formed by a two-row repeat: a row of V-stitches followed by a row of scales (or shells). This is a fairly easy pattern to execute and is fast to memorize. The only novelty about this design is that the scales are crocheted in front of the V-stitches with clusters of front post double crochets from top to bottom, then from bottom to top, as opposed to working them on top of the row like most shell patterns.

Photos used are worked with larger hook and yarn in order to show more detail.

Chain-3 at beginning of row or round counts as first double crochet unless otherwise stated.

Do not join or turn rounds unless otherwise stated.

Mark first stitch of round.

Chain-4 at beginning of row or round counts as first double crochet and chain-1 unless otherwise stated.

Join with slip stitch as indicated unless otherwise stated.

SPECIAL STITCH
V-stitch (V-st): (Dc, ch 1, dc) as indicated in instructions.

INSTRUCTIONS
CLOCHE
Rnd 1: Ch 78, being careful not to twist chain, sl st in first ch to form ring, **ch 4** *(see Pattern Notes)*, dc in same st as beg ch, *sk next 2 chs, **V-st** *(see Special Stitch)* in next ch, rep from * around, **join** *(see Pattern Notes)* in 3rd ch of beg ch-4. *(26 V-sts)*

Rnd 2: **Ch 3** *(see Pattern Notes)*, working from top to bottom around post of first dc of first V-st, work 4 **fpdc** *(see Stitch Guide and see photo A on page 27)*, ch 1, turn work so V-st is sideways and post of 2nd dc of V-st is upside down *(V point of V-st will be facing right, see photo B on page 27)*, working from bottom to top around post of 2nd dc of V-st, work 5 fpdc *(see photo C1 and C2 on page 27)*, *sk next V-st, working from top to bottom, work 5 fpdc around post of first dc of next V-st, ch 1, turn work so V-st is sideways, working from bottom to top around post of 2nd dc of V-st, work 5 fpdc, rep from * around, join in 3rd ch of beg ch-3. *(13 scales)*

A

B

C1

C2

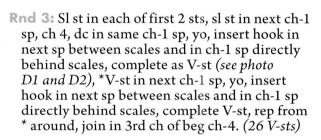

Rnd 3: Sl st in each of first 2 sts, sl st in next ch-1 sp, ch 4, dc in same ch-1 sp, yo, insert hook in next sp between scales and in ch-1 sp directly behind scales, complete as V-st *(see photo D1 and D2),* *V-st in next ch-1 sp, yo, insert hook in next sp between scales and in ch-1 sp directly behind scales, complete V-st, rep from * around, join in 3rd ch of beg ch-4. *(26 V-sts)*

D1

D2

Rnd 4: Sl st in first ch-1 sp, working from top to bottom around post of first dc of next V-st, work 5 fpdc, ch 1, turn work so V-st is sideways and post of 2nd dc of V-st is upside down, working from bottom to top around post of 2nd dc of V-st, work 5 fpdc, *sk next V-st, working from top to bottom around post of first dc of next V-st, work 5 fpdc, ch 1, turn work so V-st is sideways, working from bottom to top around post of 2nd dc of V-st, work 5 fpdc, rep from * around, join in top of beg fpdc. *(13 scales)*

Rnds 5–22: [Rep rnds 3 and 4 alternately for pattern] 9 times. There will be a total of 11 rnds of scales.

Rnd 23: Beginning top of Cloche, ch 1, *sc in each of first 2 sts, sc in next ch-1 sp, sc in each of next 2 sts, **insert hook in next sp between scales** and in ch-1 sp directly behind scales, yo, pull through and complete as sc, rep from * around, join in beg sc. *(78 sc)*

Rnd 24: [Sc in each of next 11 sc, **sc dec** *(see Pattern Notes)* in next 2 sts] around, **do not join rnds** *(see Pattern Notes)*. *(72 sc)*

Rnd 25: [Sc in each of next 10 sc, sc dec in next 2 sts] around. *(66 sc)*

Rnd 26: [Sc in each of next 9 sc, sc dec in next 2 sts] around. *(60 sc)*

Rnd 27: [Sc in each of next 8 sc, sc dec in next 2 sts] around. *(54 sc)*

Rnd 28: [Sc in each of next 7 sc, sc dec in next 2 sts] around. *(48 sc)*

Rnd 29: [Sc in each of next 6 sc, sc dec in next 2 sts] around. *(42 sc)*

Rnd 30: [Sc in each of next 5 sc, sc dec in next 2 sts] around. *(36 sc)*

Rnd 31: [Sc in each of next 4 sc, sc dec in next 2 sts] around. *(30 sc)*

Rnd 32: [Sc in each of next 3 sc, sc dec in next 2 sts] around. *(24 sc)*

Rnd 33: [Sc in each of next 2 sc, sc dec in next 2 sts] around. *(18 sc)*

Rnd 34: [Sc in next sc, sc dec in next 2 sts] around. *(12 sc)*

Last rnd: [Sc dec in next 2 sts] around. Leaving long end, fasten off. *(6 sc)*

Weave long end through top of sts on last rnd. Pull tightly to close. Secure end.

FLOWER
OPTIONAL
Rnd 1: Ch 7, sl st in first ch to form ring, [ch 10, sl st in next ch] around, join in first ch of beg ch-10 *(7 ch-10 sps)*

Rnd 2: (Sc, hdc, 8 dc, ch 2, 8 dc, hdc, sc) in first ch-10 sp and in each ch-10 sp around, join in beg sc. Fasten off. *(7 petals)*

FINISHING
Attach Flower as desired or with button sewn in center of Flower or sew on a brooch setting so it will be removable. ∎

Neck Warmer

SKILL LEVEL

INTERMEDIATE

FINISHED SIZE

6 inches wide x 22 inches long

MATERIALS

- Corny Woolness light (DK) weight yarn (3½ oz/240 yds/100g per skein):
  1 skein daylily orange

- Size G/6/4mm crochet hook or size needed to obtain gauge
- Tapestry needle
- Size 50mm/2-inch toggle button

GAUGE

3 V-sts = 2 inches; 4 V-st rows = 2 inches

PATTERN NOTES

In short, the crocodile stitch is formed by a two-row repeat: a row of V-stitches followed by a row of scales (or shells). This is a fairly easy pattern to execute and is fast to memorize. The only novelty about this design is that the scales are crocheted in front of the V-stitches with clusters of front post double crochets from top to bottom, then from bottom to top, as opposed to working them on top of the row, like in most shell patterns.

Photos used are worked with larger hook and yarn in order to show more detail.

Chain-3 at beginning of row or round counts as first double crochet unless otherwise stated.

SPECIAL STITCH

V-stitch (V-st): (Dc, ch 1, dc) as indicated in instructions.

NECK WARMER

Row 1 (WS): Ch 29, dc in 5th ch from hook *(first 4 chs and dc count as first V-st of row)*, *sk next 2 chs, **V-st** *(see Special Stitch)* in next ch, rep from * across, turn. *(9 V-sts)*

Row 2 (RS): Ch 3 *(see Pattern Notes)*, working from top to bottom around post of first dc of first V-st, work 4 **fpdc** *(see Special Stitches and photo A)*, ch 1, turn work so V-st is sideways and post of 2nd dc of V-st is upside down *(V point of V-st will be facing right, see photo B)*, working from bottom to top around post of 2nd dc of V-st, work 5 fpdc *(see photo C)*, *sk next V-st, working from top to bottom around post of first dc of next V-st, work 5 fpdc, ch 1, turn work so V-st is sideways, working from bottom to top around post of 2nd dc of V-st, work 5 fpdc, rep from * across *(see photo D)*, turn. *(5 scales)*

C

D

Row 3: Ch 3, V-st in next ch-1 sp, *yo, insert hook in next ch-1 sp and in sp between scales directly behind ch-1 sp *(see photo E)*, complete as V-st, V-st in next ch-1 sp, rep from * across to last dc, dc in last st *(see photo F)*, turn. *(9 V-sts)*

A

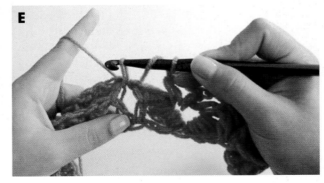

E

B

F

Row 4: Sl st in each of first 2 sts, sl st in next ch-1 sp, working from top to bottom around post of first dc of next V-st, work 5 fpdc, ch 1, turn work so V-st is sideways and post of 2nd dc of V-st is upside down, working from bottom to top around post of 2nd dc of V-st, work 5 fpdc, *sk next V-st, working from top to bottom around post of first dc of next V-st, work 5 fpdc, ch 1, turn work so V-st is sideways, working from bottom to top around post of 2nd dc of V-st, work 5 fpdc, rep from * across to last V-st, sl st in next ch-1 sp, sl st in each of next 2 sts (see photo G), turn. (4 scales)

G

Row 5: Ch 3, V-st in ch-1 sp of first V-st, *V-st in next ch-1 sp, yo, insert hook in next ch-1 sp and in sp between scales directly behind ch-1 sp, complete as V-st, V-st in next ch-1 sp, rep from * across to last ch-1 sp, V-st in last ch-1 sp, dc in last st, turn. (9 V-sts)

Row 6: Ch 1, working from top to bottom around post of first dc of first V-st, work 5 fpdc, ch 1, turn work so V-st is sideways and post of 2nd dc of V-st is upside down, working from bottom to top around post of 2nd dc of V-st, work 5 fpdc *sk next V-st, working from top to bottom around post of first dc of next V-st, work 5 fpdc, ch 1, turn work so V-st is sideways, working from bottom to top around post of 2nd dc of V-st, work 5 fpdc, rep from * across to last dc, sl st in last dc, turn. (5 scales)

Next rows: [Rep rows 3–6 consecutively] 16 times or until length of your preference.

Last row (WS): Ch 1 (counts as first sc), *sc in each of next 2 sts, sc in next ch-1 sp, sc in each of next 2 sts, insert hook in next ch-1 sp and in sp between scales directly behind ch-1 sp, yo, pull lp through and complete as sc, rep from * across to last 4 sts, sc in each of the last 4 sts. Fasten off. (29 sc)

FINISHING

Block Neck Warmer by soaking it in cool water until thoroughly wet. Gently squeeze out excess water and pin it on a flat surface. Remove it only when completely dry.

Measure about 4 inches from the top end of Neck Warmer and sew button in center scale. ∎

Slouchy Beret

SKILL LEVEL

INTERMEDIATE

FINISHED SIZE
20–22-inch head circumference

MATERIALS
- Universal Yarn Uptown Baby Sport fine (sport) weight yarn (3½ oz/ 361 yds/100g per skein):
  2 skeins #219 carolina

- Sizes F/5/3.75mm and G/6/4mm crochet hooks or sizes needed to obtain gauge
- Tapestry needle

GAUGE
Size F hook and 2 strands yarn in rib pattern:
  9 sc = 2 inches; 9 sc rows = 2 inches

Size G hook and 1 strand yarn in V-st pattern:
  3 V-sts = 2 inches; 4 V-st rows = 2 inches

PATTERN NOTES
Ribbed Band will stretch to fit range of sizes.

Ribbed Band is worked first as strip, then joined to form ring. The first round of Beret, where the scale section begins, is crocheted around row-ends of Ribbed Band.

In short, the crocodile stitch is formed by a two-row repeat: a row of V-stitches followed by a row of scales (or shells). This is a fairly easy pattern to execute and is fast to memorize. The only novelty about this design is that the scales are crocheted in front of the V-stitches with clusters of front post double crochets from top to bottom, then from bottom to top, as opposed to working them on top of the row like in most shell patterns.

Photos used are worked with larger hook and yarn in order to show more detail.

Chain-3 at beginning of row or round counts as first double crochet unless otherwise stated.

Chain-4 at beginning of row or round counts as first double crochet and chain-1 unless otherwise stated.

Join with slip stitch as indicated unless otherwise stated.

SPECIAL STITCH
V-stitch (V-st): (Dc, ch 1, dc) as indicated in instructions.

INSTRUCTIONS
BERET
RIBBED BAND
Row 1: With size F hook and holding 2 strands of yarn tog, ch 9, sc in 2nd ch from hook and in each ch across, turn. *(8 sc)*

Rows 2–60: Ch 1, working in **back lps** *(see Stitch Guide)*, sc in each sc across, turn.

Joining Ribbed Band: Hold first and last rows tog, matching sts, ch 1, working through both thicknesses, sl st in each st across. Fasten off.

Turn Ribbed Band inside out.

SCALE SECTION

Rnd 1: With RS of ribbed band facing, working in row ends around its edge, with size G hook and holding 1 strand of yarn, ch 1, evenly sp 120 sc around edge of Ribbed Band *(this equals 2 sc worked in each row-end)*, **join** *(see Pattern Notes)* in beg sc. *(120 sc)*

Rnd 2: Ch 4 *(see Pattern Notes)*, dc in same stitch as beg ch, *sk next 2 chs, **V-st** *(see Special Stitch)* in next ch, rep from * around, join in 3rd ch of beg ch-4. *(40 V-sts)*

Rnd 3: Ch 3 *(see Pattern Notes)*, working from top to bottom around post of first dc of first V-st, work 4 **fpdc** *(see Special Stitches and photo A)*, ch 1, turn work so V-st is sideways and post of 2nd dc of V-st is upside down *(V point of V-st will be facing right, see photo B)*, working from bottom to top around post of 2nd dc of V-st, work 5 fpdc *(see photo C1 and C2)*, *sk next V-st, working from top to bottom, work 5 fpdc around post of first dc of next V-st, ch 1, turn work so V-st is sideways, working from bottom to top around post of 2nd dc of V-st, work 5 fpdc, rep from * around, join in 3rd ch of beg ch-3. *(20 scales)*

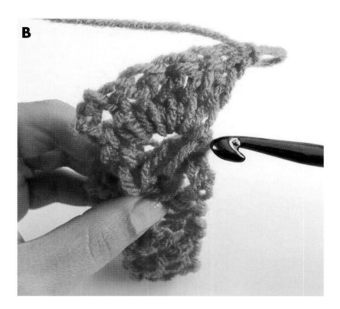

B

C1

C2

A

Rnd 4: Sl st in each of first 2 sts, sl st in next ch-1 sp, ch 4, dc in same ch-1 sp, yo, insert hook in next sp between scales and in ch-1 sp directly behind scales, complete as V-st (*see photo D1 and D2*), *V-st in next ch-1 sp, yo, insert hook in next sp between scales and in ch-1 sp directly behind scales, complete as V-st, rep from * around, join in 3rd ch of beg ch-4. (*40 V-sts*)

D1

D2

Rnd 5: Sl st in first ch-1 sp, working from top to bottom around post of first dc of next V-st, work 5 fpdc, ch 1, turn work so V-st is sideways and post of 2nd dc of V-st is upside down, working from bottom to top around post of 2nd dc of V-st, work 5 fpdc, *sk next V-st, working from top to bottom around post of first dc of next V-st, work 5 fpdc, ch 1, turn work so V-st is sideways, working from bottom to top around post of 2nd dc of V-st, work 5 fpdc, rep from * around, join in top of beg fpdc. (*20 scales*)

Rnds 6–27: [Rep rnds 4 and 5 alternately for pattern] 11 times.

Last rnd: Rep rnd 4. Leaving long end, fasten off.

There will be a total of 13 rounds of scales and a final round of V-sts.

FINISHING

Weave long end through sps of V-sts of last rnd twice, pull to gather top tightly. Secure end. ∎

Crocodile Stitch Gauntlets

SKILL LEVEL

INTERMEDIATE

FINISHED SIZES

Small/medium and large

MATERIALS

- Universal Yarn Uptown Baby Sport fine (sport) weight yarn (3½ oz/361 yds/100g per skein): 1 skein #219 carolina
- Size crochet hook needed for size and to obtain gauge

2 FINE

GAUGE

Small/medium size and size E/4/3.5mm hook: 12 V-sts = 2 inches; 5 V-st rows = 2 inches

Large size and size F/5/3.75mm hook: 10 V-sts = 2 inches; 9 V-st rows = 4 inches

PATTERN NOTES

Gauntlets are crocheted from hand to cuff.

In short, the crocodile stitch is formed by a two-row repeat: a row of V-stitches followed by a row of scales (or shells). This is a fairly easy pattern to execute and is fast to memorize. The only novelty about this design is that the scales are crocheted in front of the V-stitches with clusters of front post double crochets from top to bottom, then from bottom to top, as opposed to working them on top of the row like in most shell patterns.

Photos used are worked with larger hook and yarn in order to show more detail.

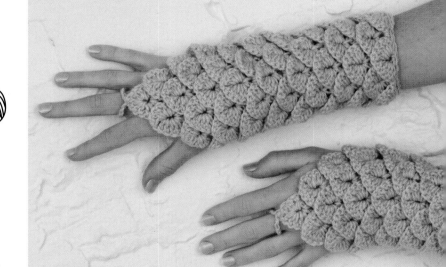

Chain-3 at beginning of row or round counts as first double crochet unless otherwise stated.

Chain-4 at beginning of row or round counts as first double crochet and chain-1 unless otherwise stated.

Join with slip stitch as indicated unless otherwise stated.

SPECIAL STITCH

V-stitch (V-st): (Dc, ch 1, dc) as indicated in instructions.

GAUNTLET
MAKE 2.

Rnd 1: Ch 6, sl st in first ch to form ring, **ch 3** *(see Pattern Notes)*, 4 dc in ring, ch 1, 5 dc in ring, **do not join and do not turn**.

This first open rnd counts as the first scale and top point of the Gauntlet, where a finger loop will be attached later.

Row 2: Now working in rows, **ch 4** *(see Pattern Notes)*, dc in same st as beg ch, **V-st** *(see Special Stitch)* in ring, V-st in last st, turn *(see photo A)*.

B1

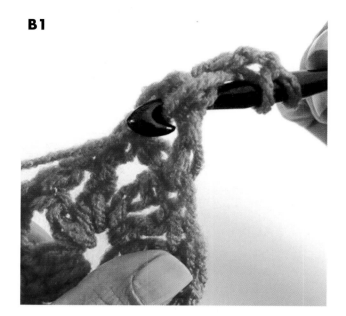

A

B2

Row 3: Ch 3, working from top to bottom around post of first dc of first V-st, work 4 **fpdc** *(see Special Stitches and photo B1 and B2)*, ch 1, turn work so V-st is sideways and post of 2nd dc of V-st is upside down *(V point of V-st will be facing right, see photo C on page 42)*, working from bottom to top around post of 2nd dc of V-st, work 5 fpdc *(see photo D on page 42)*, sk next V-st, working from top to bottom, work 5 fpdc around post of first dc of last V-st, ch 1, turn work so V-st is sideways, working from bottom to top around post of 2nd dc of V-st, work 5 fpdc *(see photo E on page 42)*, turn.

C

D

E

Row 4: Ch 4, dc in same st as beg ch, V-st in next ch-1 sp, yo, insert hook in next ch-1 sp and in sp between scales directly behind ch-1 sp *(see photo F1 and F2)*, complete as V-st, V-st in next ch-1 sp, V-st in last st, turn.

F1

F2

Row 5: Ch 3, working from top to bottom around post of first dc of first V-st, work 4 fpdc, ch 1, turn work so V-st is sideways and post of 2nd dc of V-st is upside down, working from bottom to top around post of 2nd dc of V-st, work 5 fpdc, *sk next V-st, working from top to bottom around post of first dc of next V-st, work 5 fpdc, ch 1, turn work so V-st is sideways, working from bottom to top around post of 2nd dc of V-st, work 5 fpdc, rep from * across, turn.

Row 6: Ch 4, dc in same st as beg ch, V-st in next ch-1 sp, *yo, insert hook in next ch-1 sp and in sp between scales directly behind ch-1 sp, complete as V-st, V-st in next ch-1 sp, rep from * across to last st, V-st in last st, turn.

Row 7: Rep row 5.

Row 8: Rep row 6.

Rnd 9: Now working in rnds, repeat row 5, **do not turn, join** (*see Pattern Notes*) in 3rd ch of beg ch-3 to make rnd (*see photo G*).

G

Rnd 10: Ch 4, dc in same st as beg ch, V-st in next ch-1 sp, *yo, insert hook in next sp between scales and in ch-1 sp directly behind scales, complete as V-st (*see photo H*), V-st in next ch-1 sp, rep from * around to last ch-1 sp, V-st in last ch-1 sp, join in 3rd ch of beg ch-4.

H

Rnd 11: Ch 3, working from top to bottom around post of first dc of first V-st, work 4 fpdc, ch 1, turn work so V-st is sideways and post of 2nd dc of V-st is upside down, working from bottom to top around post of 2nd dc of V-st, work 5 fpdc *sk next V-st, working from top to bottom around post of first dc of next V-st, work 5 fpdc, ch 1, turn work so V-st is sideways, working from bottom to top around post of 2nd dc of V-st, work 5 fpdc, rep from * around, join in 3rd ch of beg ch-3.

Rnd 12: Sl st in each of first 2 sts, sl st in next ch-1 sp, ch 4, dc in same ch-1 sp, yo, insert hook in next sp between scales and in ch-1 sp directly behind scales, complete as V-st, * V-st in next ch-1 sp, yo, insert hook in next sp between scales and in ch-1 sp directly behind scales, complete as V-st, rep from * around, join in 3rd ch of beg ch-4.

Rnd 13: Sl st in first ch-1 sp, working from top to bottom around post of first dc of next V-st, work 5 fpdc, ch 1, turn work so V-st is sideways and post of 2nd dc of V-st is upside down, working from bottom to top around post of 2nd dc of V-st, work 5 fpdc, *sk next V-st, working from top to bottom around post of first dc of next V-st, work 5 fpdc, ch 1, turn work so V-st is sideways, working from bottom to top around post of 2nd dc of V-st, work 5 fpdc, rep from * around, join in beg fpdc.

Rnds 14–33: [Rep rnds 12 and 13 alternately] 10 times.

Rnd 34: Rep rnd 12.

Last rnd: Ch 1, *sc in each of next 2 sts, sc in next ch-1 sp, sc in each of next 2 sts, insert hook in next sp between scales and in ch-1 sp directly behind scales, yo, pull lp through and complete as sc, rep from * around, join in beg sc. Fasten off.

FINGER LOOP
Join in ch-1 of rnd 1, ch 14 or ch long enough to circle around your middle finger comfortably, sl st in same ch-1 to join Finger Loop. Fasten off. ∎

projects

STITCH GUIDE

STITCH ABBREVIATIONS

beg ....begin/begins/beginning
bpdc ....back post double crochet
bpsc ....back post single crochet
bptr ....back post treble crochet
CC ....contrasting color
ch(s) ....chain(s)
ch- ....refers to chain or space
previously made (i.e., ch-1 space)
ch sp(s) ....chain space(s)
cl(s) ....cluster(s)
cm ....centimeter(s)
dc .... double crochet (singular/plural)
dc dec............... double crochet 2 or more
stitches together, as indicated
dec...................... decrease/decreases/decreasing
dtr .... double treble crochet
ext ....extended
fpdc .... front post double crochet
fpsc .... front post single crochet
fptr .... front post treble crochet
g ....gram(s)
hdc .... half double crochet
hdc dec .... half double crochet 2 or more
stitches together, as indicated
inc .... increase/increases/increasing
lp(s) ....loop(s)
MC ....main color
mm ....millimeter(s)
oz ....ounce(s)
pc ....popcorn(s)
rem .... remain/remains/remaining
rep(s) ....repeat(s)
rnd(s) ....round(s)
RS ....right side
sc .... single crochet (singular/plural)
sc dec...................single crochet 2 or more
stitches together, as indicated
sk ....skip/skipped/skipping
sl st(s) ....slip stitch(es)
sp(s) ....space(s)/spaced
st(s) ....stitch(es)
tog ....together
tr..treble crochet
trtr...triple treble
WS ....wrong side
yd(s) ....yard(s)
yo ....yarn over

YARN CONVERSION

OUNCES TO GRAMS	GRAMS TO OUNCES
1.............28.4	25 ....⅞
2.............56.7	40 ....1⅔
3.............85.0	50 ....1¾
4.............113.4	100...........3½

UNITED STATES		UNITED KINGDOM
sl st (slip stitch)	=	sc (single crochet)
sc (single crochet)	=	dc (double crochet)
hdc (half double crochet)	=	htr (half treble crochet)
dc (double crochet)	=	tr (treble crochet)
tr (treble crochet)	=	dtr (double treble crochet)
dtr (double treble crochet)	=	ttr (triple treble crochet)
skip	=	miss

Reverse single crochet (reverse sc): Ch 1, sk first st, working from left to right, insert hook in next st from front to back, draw up lp on hook, yo, and draw through both lps on hook.

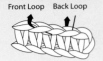

Chain (ch): Yo, pull through lp on hook.

Single crochet (sc): Insert hook in st, yo, pull through st, yo, pull through both lps on hook.

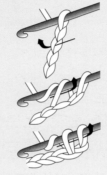

Double crochet (dc): Yo, insert hook in st, yo, pull through st, [yo, pull through 2 lps] twice.

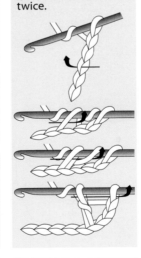

Front loop (front lp) Back loop (back lp)

Front Loop   Back Loop

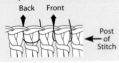

Front post stitch (fp): Back post stitch (bp): When working post st, insert hook from right to left around post of st on previous row.

Back   Front

Post of Stitch

Half double crochet (hdc): Yo, insert hook in st, yo, pull through st, yo, pull through all 3 lps on hook.

Double treble crochet (dtr): Yo 3 times, insert hook in st, yo, pull through st, [yo, pull through 2 lps] 4 times.

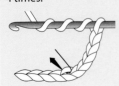

Slip stitch (sl st): Insert hook in st, pull through both lps on hook.

Chain color change (ch color change) Yo with new color, draw through last lp on hook.

Double crochet color change (dc color change) Drop first color, yo with new color, draw through last 2 lps of st.

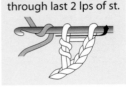

Treble crochet (tr): Yo twice, insert hook in st, yo, pull through st, [yo, pull through 2 lps] 3 times.

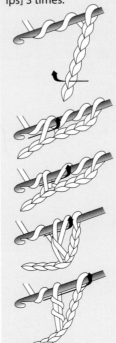

Single crochet decrease (sc dec): (Insert hook, yo, draw lp through) in each of the sts indicated, yo, draw through all lps on hook.

Example of 2-sc dec

Half double crochet decrease (hdc dec): (Yo, insert hook, yo, draw lp through) in each of the sts indicated, yo, draw through all lps on hook.

Example of 2-hdc dec

Double crochet decrease (dc dec): (Yo, insert hook, yo, draw lp through, yo, draw through 2 lps on hook) in each of the sts indicated, yo, draw through all lps on hook.

Example of 2-dc dec

Treble crochet decrease (tr dec): Holding back last lp of each st, tr in each of the sts indicated, yo, pull through all lps on hook.

Example of 2-tr dec

Metric Conversion Charts

METRIC CONVERSIONS

yards	x	.9144	=	metres (m)
yards	x	91.44	=	centimetres (cm)
inches	x	2.54	=	centimetres (cm)
inches	x	25.40	=	millimetres (mm)
inches	x	.0254	=	metres (m)

centimetres	x	.3937	=	inches
metres	x	1.0936	=	yards

INCHES INTO MILLIMETRES & CENTIMETRES (Rounded off slightly)

inches	mm	cm	inches	cm	inches	cm	inches	cm
1/8	3	0.3	5	12.5	21	53.5	38	96.5
1/4	6	0.6	5 1/2	14	22	56	39	99
3/8	10	1	6	15	23	58.5	40	101.5
1/2	13	1.3	7	18	24	61	41	104
5/8	15	1.5	8	20.5	25	63.5	42	106.5
3/4	20	2	9	23	26	66	43	109
7/8	22	2.2	10	25.5	27	68.5	44	112
1	25	2.5	11	28	28	71	45	114.5
1 1/4	32	3.2	12	30.5	29	73.5	46	117
1 1/2	38	3.8	13	33	30	76	47	119.5
1 3/4	45	4.5	14	35.5	31	79	48	122
2	50	5	15	38	32	81.5	49	124.5
2 1/2	65	6.5	16	40.5	33	84	50	127
3	75	7.5	17	43	34	86.5		
3 1/2	90	9	18	46	35	89		
4	100	10	19	48.5	36	91.5		
4 1/2	115	11.5	20	51	37	94		

KNITTING NEEDLES CONVERSION CHART

Canada/U.S.	0	1	2	3	4	5	6	7	8	9	10	10½	11	13	15
Metric (mm)	2	2¼	2¾	3¼	3½	3¾	4	4½	5	5½	6	6½	8	9	10

CROCHET HOOKS CONVERSION CHART

Canada/U.S.	1/B	2/C	3/D	4/E	5/F	6/G	8/H	9/I	10/J	10½/K	N
Metric (mm)	2.25	2.75	3.25	3.5	3.75	4.25	5	5.5	6	6.5	9.0

Crocodile Stitch Fashions is published by DRG, 306 East Parr Road, Berne, IN 46711. Printed in USA. Copyright © 2011 DRG.

RETAIL STORES: If you would like to carry this pattern book or any other DRG publications, visit DRGwholesale.com.

Every effort has been made to ensure that the instructions in this publication are complete and accurate.
We cannot, however, take responsibility for human error, typographical mistakes or variations in individual work.
Please visit AnniesCustomerCare.com to check for pattern updates.

ISBN: 978-1-59635-397-8

3 4 5 6 7 8 9